Mastering Bitcoin:

The Ultimate Guide for Beginners to Understanding Bitcoin Technology, Bitcoin Investing, Bitcoin Mining and other Cryptocurrencies.

2nd Edition

Anthony Tu

information contained within this document, including, but not limited to, —errors, omissions, or inaccuracies

For more information, go to www.wonpublications.com

Table of Contents

About the Author

Anthony Tu (also known as Anthony Tuanga) is a computer scientist, author and a cryptocurrency investor. He has been working in the field of computer science for the last 10 years and completed his degree at Harvard University. He came across cryptocurrencies early in 2011 and fell in love with the technology.

He is a large investor in cryptocurrencies such as Bitcoin, Ethereum and continues to share his vast knowledge in the space.

Outside of work, he is a family man. He loves to spend time with his beautiful wife and son.

Introduction

I want to thank you for choosing and purchasing this book, *'Mastering Bitcoin: The Ultimate Guide for Beginners to Understanding Bitcoin Technology, Bitcoin Investing, Bitcoin Mining and Other Cryptocurrencies."*

In this book, you'll find everything you need to know about Bitcoin, from the history of Bitcoin, to the nitty gritty side of Bitcoin Mining. This book will be your ultimate guide and something you can refer to now, and in the future. As a BONUS, not only is this book about the essentials of Bitcoin, information about other Cryptocurrencies will be added for your benefit.

If you're like me, you would've heard about Bitcoin somewhere, possibly from a friend, the news, or even the fact that you just wanted to find new ways to make money. I was all the above. Before I started investing into cryptocurrencies, I invested in traditional stocks and bonds, but I realized that it simply wasn't exciting enough. I heard of Bitcoin every now and then, I read that people have been making hundreds of thousands and even MILLIONS on Bitcoin, but I didn't believe it. It wasn't until my friend told me that he made $2000 profit on a $500 investment on Bitcoin that I was blown away. I know what you might be thinking, this isn't that much right? Keeping in mind, this was when we were 21 and he had only invested in Bitcoin for about a year. Traditional investments such as stocks, only make about 8% per year on average, so to obtain a 400% return on investment was mind blowing. I didn't know what Bitcoin really was or what the functions and practical uses were, but I was curious enough to research it and once I dove right into the world of cryptocurrencies, I realized the absolute potential that Bitcoin and the other altcoins (alternative cryptocurrencies) possess.

I know you are excited to learn about Bitcoin, and we'll get started in a second. Again, I'd like to thank you for choosing this book. I have comprised everything I know about Bitcoin in my years of experience, and I know you'll enjoy this book. This is the beginning of your cryptocurrency adventure and I hope you're as excited as I am.

At the end of this book, you'll be given a FREE step-by-step course so that you can start investing in Bitcoin today!

Let's get started!

For easy understanding, we will start from the very beginning of bitcoins and cryptocurrencies.

Chapter 1: Basics of Cryptocurrency

Cryptocurrency is the name given to any digital currency that is deemed secure because of cryptography — or a particular kind of encryption method that's perfect for the whole blockchain process. What's amazing about cryptocurrencies is that no central authorities govern them. They are organic and are a perfect system on their own. The government or anyone not involved in Blockchain cannot manipulate them in any way— keeping your funds always in check. In fact, it is virtually impossible for any governing body to track down any transactions and associate it to an individual. This is what makes cryptocurrencies so fascinating and why some governments are highly against cryptocurrencies.

One thing about cryptocurrency transactions is that they might be used for illicit activities — such as tax evasion or even money laundering. Prior to larger adoption in 2017, particularly the early years, there has been a lot of controversy about the uses of cryptocurrencies, that it is only used for activity done on dark web, including drug dealings.

This is different in 2017 where there has been a larger acceptance of cryptocurrencies, with some banks incorporating the Blockchain technology and various companies accepting cryptocurrencies as a form of payment. The main argument towards cryptocurrencies is the ability for parties to easily send and accept funds from each other, even in cryptocurrency form, and only with minimal transaction fees. There are also many other uses for cryptocurrency, including crowdfunding and online voting. After all, people find it easier to spend online currencies instead of real ones— they don't cause too much hassle either.

Cryptocurrency is money created by the use of encryption techniques of advanced computer programming. These same techniques are used to carry out and verify the transfer of funds. Cryptocurrencies are independent of central banks and are decentralized. This means that parties can send and receive funds directly towards each other without a middleman. For most people, sending money is a hassle, particularly when you want to send money abroad. If you're transferring money between local banks, it could potentially take days for the banks to clear and verify the transactions to be made. When sending abroad, this is a different case; in certain situations this could take more than a week, let alone the fees of processing the transactions. Some major companies like Western Union allow faster transactions, but it comes at a cost, the fees.

The implications of cryptocurrency are so great that some central banks have attempted to involve themselves in the technology, with some attempting to issue their own cryptocurrencies. However, the currency they produce is not officially considered cryptocurrency as they can only develop centralized money. The idea behind decentralization is to allow the open market to influence the power. With centralization, all the power and control is with the centralized body, the central banks, meaning that you and I have no say in how much money is created or what it's worth. In this sense, the Federal Reserve can manipulate the value of traditional currencies (i.e US Dollar) via printing more money and there's nothing we can do. The proponents of cryptocurrency are very keen on keeping the "true" digital currency decentralized and because of this, cryptocurrencies have seen to be very favorable. Because of the unique nature of cryptocurrencies, is it actually deflationary, as time goes on, the value of most cryptocurrencies will go higher.

Rise of Cryptocurrency

Cryptocurrencies, such as Bitcoin, Ethereum, Litecoin and others, have had a lot of publicity, particularly in 2017. This is primarily due to the large exposure given by the news, social media and financial institutions. As the levels of financial/digital literacy of the general population have increased, cryptocurrency acceptance has also made leaps in purchasing power. In 2010, a Bitcoin investor, known as Laslo, claimed to have purchased two pizzas for roughly 10,000 Bitcoins. It was considered the first instance where a cryptocurrency was used to make a purchase. At the time, Bitcoins were virtually worthless. As of November 2017, Bitcoin is valued higher than gold, with one-coin worth nearly $10,000!

At first, most were very skeptical of Bitcoin and its technology, seeing it as a form of counterfeit or a device of criminals. This was particularly so when it was publicized as the means of trade on the 'Silk Road,' a part of the dark Internet where all sorts of unsavory behavior were rampant.

However, there is now an increasing involvement of legitimate business and government with cryptocurrency. New applications and even ATM's are incorporated to allow cryptocurrency transactions to occur. As a consequence, the market capitalization of all cryptocurrencies is more than $250,000,000,000!

By Mid 2017, we have seen a rise in cryptocurrencies, revealing more than 1000 cryptocurrencies. Most people have heard of Bitcoin, especially since recent ransomware attacks have demanded payment in Bitcoins. The benefit to criminals of this is that any such payment by a victim would be untraceable.

If the website for coinmarketcap is checked, it will be seen that there is a small graph beside the type of cryptocurrency, each showing the movement of the currency in the last week, as well as the percentage change in the last 24 hours. It will be seen that there is a significant disparity in the values of the various cryptocurrencies with one Bitcoin being worth nearly $10,000 and a total market capitalization of more than $150,000,000,000. Another cryptocurrency called Bytecoin was worth less than one cent although the total capitalization of Bytecoins was more than $200,000,000. Some cryptocurrencies have small capitalizations. An example is MikeTheMug cryptocurrency with a capitalization of approximately $1000!

Just reading this, you may be wondering how a coin like 'MikeTheMug' can be taken seriously, and with all due respect for MikeTheMug, it is actually easier than most people think to create and issue a coin, which makes some individuals quite skeptical about cryptocurrencies.

Though there are a lot of valid and exciting potential projects within cryptocurrencies, it should be noted there are also a lot of 'joke' coins with no actual fundamental value. A good example is Dogecoin that I myself do find quite hysterical, however, the coin itself serves no real purpose aside from representing the patriotism that society has created through hysterical memes and the Internet. To put that in perspective, Dogecoin has a market cap of more than $200,000,000, based on a meme of a dog.

We will have more to say about the quality and worth of cryptocurrencies later.

Cryptocurrency as Money

The people involved in cryptocurrency call the currencies we use, in everyday life, 'fiat', or 'fiat currency' Despite the word 'currency' in the word cryptocurrency, there are greater similarities between cryptocurrencies and stocks than cryptocurrencies and fiat currencies. A purchase of some cryptocurrency is similarly a purchase of a technology stock, an entry in a digital ledger called a blockchain, and a part of the digital network for that cryptocurrency. Buying cryptocurrencies is similarly to stock purchasing because each 'cryptocurrency' represents a different project. When you purchase these cryptocurrencies, you're buying a share within the project. An example of which is Ethereum or Ether. Having Ether allows the investor to participate in voting within the Ethereum network.

Cryptocurrency is a means of exchange that uses cryptography so that transactions are secure. They are used to exercise control over the manufacture of further units of the currency. Cryptocurrencies are a type of what is called alternative currencies; different from traditional currencies such as everyone is familiar with, the US Dollar, the Euro, the British Pound, etc.

Due to their frequent and great fluctuations in value, one of the two fundamentals of money, namely "a store of value" is lacking. Within any new markets, there are large fluctuations in the prices of the assets. But as the market begins to grow over time, you will see price stability as well as more institutional and commercial uses. A good example is the stock market within periods of recessions, where uncertainty generally leads to large fluctuations in prices. However, most of the time, the prices of the large capitalization companies in the stock market are fairly stable. Within the cryptocurrency market, Bitcoin is starting to unfold as the most stable cryptocurrency.

Quite ironically, Bitcoin was initially released to allow decentralized peer-to-peer transactions to take place, but because of the explosive popularity of Bitcoin in recent years,

Bitcoin has seen to become more of a store value due to ridiculous costs to transfer Bitcoin in between wallets. A lot of individuals see Bitcoin as the gold standard within the cryptocurrency world, and much like gold is to be held, a lot of investors choose to hold Bitcoin within the cryptocurrency market. Some digital currencies exhibit the behavior of countries having significant inflation in that value is not retained.

Chapter 1: History of Bitcoin

The Creation of Cryptocurrency

So as we know, 'cryptocurrency' is the name given to any digital currencies encrypted through a method known as 'cryptography'. One of the first known descriptions of Cryptocurrency comes from Wei Dai in 1998. Most of these currencies during this time were represented by the computer "bit" size. This is likely why you get names like b-money and Bit Gold in the early works of cryptocurrency. Most of Bitcoin was created before Bitcoin existed, such as the famous Proof of Work concept (which will be covered further on) that Bitcoin is currently famous for is a part of Bit Gold. However, nothing really caught on until Bitcoin was created in 2009.

The Failed Currencies before Bitcoin

Wei Dai created the description of b-money but it is undocumented as to whether it was ever put into action. Bit Gold, on the other hand, was physically created by Nick Szabo but, like b-money, was never put into action either. It is often suspected that Szabo was the creator of Bitcoin due to how similar Bit Gold was to Bitcoin (heck, even the name sounds similar) but Nick always refused to lay claim to the program. 1994 brought the year where the EU started regulating Prepaid Cards and this, unintentionally, killed a lot of ideas that involved cryptocurrency. Shortly after, we received the great gift we called PayPal. PayPal was the first step towards cryptocurrency and as PayPal's became more successful, so did the demand for internet money. Welcome Bitcoin.

11

The Creation of Bitcoin: Satoshi Nakamoto

In 2009, Bitcoin became the first practicable cryptocurrency, proving that a decentralized currency could exist. This is ironic; given that Bitcoin inventor Satoshi Nakamoto never set out to create a new form of money. He wanted to solve the problem of centralized digital cash and created a peer-to-peer digital cash system. He ended up developing Bitcoin, an entirely unregulated form of currency, which relied upon extensive mathematical computations to validate authenticity. It was with the birth of Bitcoin that cryptocurrency became a reality, forever changing how we do transactions.

In 2008, the Satoshi paper was released and the idea of Bitcoin was released in an academic paper titled "Bitcoin: A Peer to Peer Electronic Cash System". Satoshi, who was an anonymous user on that forum, began to circulate their ideas around. The known release of Bitcoin became popular around 2009. Satoshi Nakamoto released the first version of the Bitcoin software (Version 0.1) on 9th January, 2009. The Bitcoin website was created with its domain name as bitcoin.org. From there on, Satoshi went a step ahead to work in partnership with other software developers to improve the Bitcoin software until around the middle of the year 2010. It was until this time that Satoshi announced his departure and transferred control of the network alert key and code base (source code) of the Bitcoin software to Gavin Andresen.

Andresen stated afterwards that he sought to decentralize the functioning of Bitcoin.

"As soon as Satoshi stepped back and threw the project on my shoulders, one of the things I did was to decentralize that. So if I get hit by a bus," he joked, "it would be clear that the project would go on".

The idea behind Bitcoin was to create a peer to peer, decentralized system where two individuals can send each other transactions without any authorization. This means that if person A wanted to send person B Bitcoin, they could do it without any governing body, like a bank or an external company such as Western Union. The main aim of creating Bitcoin was to come up with a form of currency that cannot be controlled by businesses or governments in that it allows you to conduct trade without having to reveal your identity or having to pay any additional costs.

Once it landed on the market, the Bitcoin market seemed to slowly crawl at first before exploding in 2014, skyrocketing to a value of $1,000 as a market value for a single BTC. The spike in the prices of Bitcoin varied greatly, particularly in 2017, where the prices surged higher than $10,000 for 1 Bitcoin! As of 15th January 2018, 1 bitcoin is worth $13, 938.

The Problems of Bitcoin

There are a few issues with Bitcoin that do not make themselves apparent very quickly. The first problem is that all transactions have no physical middleman, which means that no government can look at all the transactions currently happening. That's not a problem until you realize that everything that used to be difficult to exchange with paper money become all too easy with Bitcoin. The fact that trade transactions cannot be traced back to you makes it a dream come true for money launderers, terrorists, extortionists, cyber criminals and drug dealers. Essentially, that means you can digitally buy drugs with

Bitcoin without government interference and the government can't track what Bitcoin is funding.

There are also concerns that unlike all other investment avenues available, bitcoin and other forms of cryptocurrencies are not regulated by central banks or government entities. There isn't any authority you can approach to air your grievances. For instance, if you purchase something with your credit card and get duped, you could always contact your bank and demand for compensation or solve that issue amicably. But what do you think can happen if you get duped in a bitcoin transaction? Do you think no matter what you do you will get your money back? Herein lies the problem of investing through such unregulated schemes.

The other problem is that Bitcoin is the new Gold Standard because there will only ever be a certain amount of Bitcoins available on the market, which means that Bitcoin value will continue rise until it is near unattainable for everyone. This will only happen if the community retains hoarders. The third problem I see, because there could be far more that I don't know about, is the immediate devaluing of current currencies. What happens when the dollar is no longer the reserve income of the world? Where will the trillions of dollars' worth of debt go? The U.S.A. isn't the only country like this either because you have countries with even bigger debts such as Japan, Lebanon, Greece, and Italy. Let's say that Japan gathers ten million Bitcoins (a rough half of all those that will ever exist). Speculators have said the Bitcoin price could go up to $100,000 a BTC. It wouldn't be difficult for Japan to do this either and that's one trillion dollars just so you know. What happens if Japan sells all of those Bitcoins for the USD? That would be a massive economic shift that everyone would feel because when money leaves the country, it puts that country further into debt with the rest of the world. It must now back that trillion dollars that just left

14

the country. It is only when the country brings in money with sold products that it pays off debt and since BTC is a product, it would effectively shift one trillion dollars' worth of debt from Japan to the U.S.A.

Another problem is that once Bitcoin transactions are completed they cannot be reversed. And this can prove to be a huge problem especially if the whole transaction process later proves to be a sham. Cyber criminals have identified this problem and come up with strategies to make the most of such a situation. They are circulating malware (malicious softwares) around the internet that roam and scan people's hard disks searching for bitcoins. Unfortunately for you, if your computer is not secured from such malware and you happen to posses' unencrypted bitcoins in your hard drive, then you risk losing all of them at once without your consent.

Similarly, because of how the Bitcoin was designed, if anyone were to gain access to your 'private key' (password), then that person not only has access to all your bitcoins he/she has the authorization to spend them in whatever way he/she wishes. Just in the same way a robber comes to steal a stack of money that you keep under your bed; a cyber criminal can steal your digital private key and use it to spend your bitcoins.

Fortunately for bitcoin users, there are various countermeasures that you can take to prevent being on the receiving end of such actions. For example, if you have a sizeable amount of bitcoins in your possession, you are advised to move them all to a 'cold storage' (a flash drive or hard disk that is not connected to any computer connected to the internet and then hidden in a secure location such as a physical safe. Currently, bitcoin developers are still working on a new software patch to address the same problem. They are trying to come up with a technology known as the **multi signature**

transactions that will not submit a transaction to the network before two or more people sign and clear it for approval.

Let's take our discussion about bitcoin a bit further.

Chapter 2: Understanding Bitcoin

Bitcoin is digital or virtual money. Created in 2009, bitcoin became the first decentralized digital currency, which works without the control of a central authority e.g., a central bank. The bitcoin network is peer to peer and the transactions that take place within the network take place between individual users without any intermediary. When a transaction is initiated, it is verified by a network of computers (known as nodes) with the use of cryptocurrency after which the transaction is recorded in a public distributed ledger referred to as blockchain. Bitcoins are not like the physical coins you have in your wallet or purse. They are basically coded language, a line of digital 0's and 1's that are used in computer programming. They are however similar to tangible currency in that once you acquire them, you can buy anything with them or exchange them for services or even normal currency.

Fiat Money

A lot of people have a hard time wrapping their head around Bitcoin but the honest truth is that Bitcoin is not that different from our actual physical money. Did you know the World's Reserve Dollar represents the most basic form of a Fiat money? A Fiat money has its value determined by the people rather than by the value of another object. For instance, the U.S. dollar is backed by an estimated value but in the past, it has been backed by the gold standard or, rather, the worth gold stood for (fiat on top of fiat, you could say). The gold standard means that a certain portion of money represents a very specific amount of gold. Many countries start off with the gold standard and move on from it, but many people believe that the gold standard helps control economics and wish to go back to it. The problem with gold is that it simply acts as a middleman for fiat money and so money would do the same thing with or without gold. The only way for money to stabilize, to some, is to simply stop printing more money. However, because it's no longer representing gold as a value and it has a value of its own, this now becomes a Fiat money. Bitcoin is similar in that the value of Bitcoin is set by the market or, rather, how much someone is willing to spend in order to gain access to Bitcoin.

Bitcoin Is Similar To Gold; But Way Better

Bitcoin shares many similarities with gold and one common characteristic they share is that they both have a finite supply. It is not possible to simply pull gold in arbitrary quantities from thin air. You have to mine or extract it from the ground and thereafter supply it into the market for circulation depending on the market prices. The problem with the gold standard is that it actually gets in the way of the banking capability to give out fiduciary media.

Bitcoin therefore has been credited with taking the benefits that gold brings a notch higher, the only difference is that it is digital.

Gold as you know not only takes a lot of physical space but it is also very heavy and that is why if you are under the gold standard, you will prefer to substitute the gold for paper. This system ensures that the gold is left in the banks and you put your faith in the bank that it will handle your gold responsibly. Therefore, even when the strict gold standard becomes more strict, some of these financial institutions are tempted to betray their clients' trust by making new deposits and giving out fiduciary media.

But then the savior in the mould of Bitcoin came along. Since it operates on a digital platform, it takes up no physical space and also costs next to nothing to store unlike its predecessor. As a result, you can carry bitcoin with you anywhere in the world without an extra load. And better still, you don't even need paper substitutes for your bitcoins and neither will there be any need to give the banks an opportunity to take money from you. And just like you can break down gold into small units for carrying around, bitcoin is even better, as it has its own units, which means anyone who wants to invest in bitcoins can afford it with a lot of ease.

Common Bitcoin Measurement Units

The way you can break down a €100 (a hundred euro) note/bill into 100 €1 coins is the same way you can also break down 1 bitcoin (the currency abbreviated as BTC like USD is for the American dollar) into smaller units. Since the value of the bitcoin is gradually soaring from time to time (as of 15th January 2018, 1 bitcoin is worth $13, 938), the prices of many commodities in the market have to be displayed as an alternative metric system of denomination in fractional bitcoin currency.

For example, the value of one ink pen can be 0.001 BTC. The problem is that such fractional numerical prices can be a bit complicated or confusing to read. To make the reading much easier, we can convert the bitcoin to the **bit** sub unit (1 bit = 0.000001 bitcoins). In this case, the aforementioned pen will cost 1000 bits. You can now see that such use of the fractional bitcoin currencies makes the reading of bitcoin prices much more intuitive and also very memorable.

The main aim of the bitcoin currency (BTC) is to ensure that it forges harmony with the rest of all the other currencies globally. To accomplish this goal therefore, the creators of bitcoin ensured that a single bitcoin could be divisible all the way down to the 8th decimal place. In figures, this translates to 0.00000001 BTC or $^1/_{100000000}$ BTC. Likewise, 1 bitcoin is equal to 1 million bits.

The smallest denomination or unit of the bitcoin is the satoshi, which is just but homage that recognizes the founding father of the Bitcoin protocol, Satoshi Nakamoto. the 2nd smallest sub unit is known as the finney. It was also names after Hal Finney, a man who is considered to be one of bitcoin's first pioneers and also made contact with Satoshi.

The table below shows the list of the bitcoin metric system of denominations; all the way from the largest (BTC) to the least in value (satoshi).

#	DENOMINATION	ABBREVIATION	FAMILIAR NAME	VALUE IN BTC
1	Bitcoin	BTC	Bitcoin	1
2	Decibit	dBTC	Deci-bitcoin	0.1
3	Centibit	cBTC	Centi-bitcoin	0.01
4	Millibit	mBTC	Milli-bitcoin	0.001
5	Bit (Microbit)	µBTC	Bit (Micro-bitcoin)	0.000001
6	Finney	FIN	Finney	0.0000001
7	Satoshi	SAT	Satoshi	0.00000001

I know you might be wondering; so how do people arrive at the prices that you see on the news? Let's discuss that next.

How Is The Value Of Bitcoin Determined?

The value of 1 bitcoin is largely dependent on the supply and demand theory. In simple terms, the value is determined by fluctuations of the market just as is the case with all other currencies. If the demand for bitcoins increases or if the supply reduces, then the value of a bitcoin increases and the reverse is also true. Nevertheless, the bitcoin was created to always appreciate in terms of value as time elapses. And this is the reason why it has such a big number of denominations. New bitcoins are released into the market at an estimated rate of 1 new coin every 24 seconds. Up to date, there are around 16 million bitcoins circulating since the first ever coins were introduced in the year 2009. The bitcoin system is different from the traditional currencies in that the reserve of bitcoins is fixed. But the supply of bitcoins will eventually stop as this system has been programmed to ensure that only a total of an exact 21 million bitcoins can ever be in circulation.

If this is the case, then calculations show that around the year 2140, all the available 21 million bitcoins will be in circulation and there won't be any free coins left in the store to extract as rewards from mining. By this point, the Bitcoin currency will have appreciated to immeasurable proportions and this is the reason why it was broken down into many sub units. In this respect, if the worth of a solitary bitcoin multiplies by thousands or millions of dollars, then you will still be able to use it to purchase the cheapest commodity available on the internet.

We've mentioned cryptocurrency multiple times in the book. What exactly is cryptocurrency?

Cryptocurrency

Cryptocurrency is refers to the name given to all digital currencies encrypted through cryptography. If you think of all the physical currencies (US dollar, Australian dollar, Japanese Yen, Euro, etc.), what separates these physical currencies from cryptocurrencies is digitization. This means you can't physically hold cryptocurrencies, such as Bitcoin. You can think of Bitcoin as the dollar and other big players like Ethereum and Litecoin as other currencies.

The term 'Cryptocurrency' isn't all that new; it was actually available to us in the 1980s, but only recently have we developed a method to where we can utilize cryptocurrency and validate the worth of the currency. You see, previous cryptocurrencies relied on single transfer computers and this caused an issue known as the double spending problem. In reality, you had no way of proving that the currency that you obtained was lawfully obtained and not just created on your computer via copy and paste. Since most cryptocurrencies were from public sources and could be recreated, we simply couldn't trust cryptocurrency but with Bitcoin, the story changed. Bitcoin works as a peer-to-peer connection in that everyone has a validating key that determines how many Bitcoins are on the market at the time and who has those Bitcoins. If your Bitcoin isn't one of those Bitcoins when it is validated against the system, it is seen as a fake and this provides validity and trustworthiness in the Bitcoin system. You have a public key, which is what you share with everybody else whenever you want to spend or receive Bitcoins and then you have the private key, which is what is used whenever the transaction occurs to validate your Bitcoins. This simplistic process allows for the validation of the Bitcoins and since the top Security Experts in the world have said that such a system is trustworthy, we now recognize Bitcoin as a vetted cryptocurrency.

How Encryption Makes The Use Of Cryptocurrencies Secure

You already know that cryptocurrencies such as Ethereum and Bitcoin use a peer to peer decentralized system to carry out transactions. And given the fact that all this is done online, some concerns were raised that such transactions might be volatile or worse still prone to cyber attacks from hackers. Now you need not worry about any of these because cryptocurrencies use cryptography to ensure that whatever transactions you carry out are secured to the highest degree.

Cryptography from an Information technology point of view is associated with the process of securing electronic information in the presence adversaries (of malicious 3rd parties) when communicating. This is done by encryption (converting the readable text into cipher text (text format that is unreadable)). The cipher text can only be reconverted back to readable text only by use of a special secret key and an algorithm. A particular algorithm will always convert the same readable text into cipher text and vice versa if the same key is used. Any algorithm is secure to use for encryption provided that a hacker will be unable to determine the properties of readable text or the key even after obtaining the cipher text.

Problems with Old Cryptocurrency

Cryptocurrency does have a few problems with it due to the fact that there are several inconsistencies that naturally occur with money. The first problem is that there are several different types of cryptocurrencies. As I've already said, we've had the technology since the 1980s. It has only been in recent history that we have had some success with Bitcoin and this means that there are going to be several different types of cryptocurrencies available for you to get. The second problem is an additional effect with having more than one type of currency. Due to the fact that there are several different types of cryptocurrencies, the variation in value constantly changes all the time. This means that sometimes Bitcoin will be the most valued but other times it may be more effective to farm a new type of cryptocurrency.

Another problem is that the processing speed of cryptocurrency transactions like that of bitcoin is usually slow. The slow nature is due to the protection of the blockchains that make such cryptocurrencies very secure. Again, since there is also a limit to the number of transactions that can be carried out in a single day, it might take even days let alone hours to finalize a simple transaction.

Last of all, you always run the risk that the cryptocurrency that you are investing in or trading in is going to bubble and bust and this just comes with any type of natural money but with cryptocurrency, you definitely shouldn't start out by investing everything you own in it because you don't know if the cryptocurrency is going to be worth anything within the next week.

What Bitcoin Fixes

There are a few things that cryptocurrency actually fixes that a lot of banks have problems with and the first of this is the country boundary that has almost always applied to paper money in the past. You see, there are fees included with changing any type of money to any type of money but there are some countries where the change simply isn't possible. For example, companies such as MoneyGram or Western Union charge rates of about 8% to send money from one country to another. Due to the fact that Bitcoin is a universal money, the fees that are applied are simply the fees that are incurred if you go with a service. If you were to trade with someone on a personal level, there's no middle man such as a bank, stocking trade company, or any other type of middleman person that would normally charge you a fee for such an exchange. On a personal level, you can simply hand them Bitcoin and then receive a product without having to pay sales tax or anything like that. Additionally, you have some countries that don't have access to American Banks or things like PayPal and Bitcoin helps overcome this challenge because it bypasses the link, the bureaucratic process of getting a country approved for utilizing another country's type of currency.

Bitcoin is also determined to save people who have to go through dysfunctional banking systems in developing countries. The problem with the conventional banking systems is that they are geographically isolated. This means that if you are an Argentine for instance, you are only expected to use the Argentinean banking system and the same goes to all other countries as well. However, this is the bridge that Bitcoin is looking to gap because its network is global. This benefits mostly the people living in the low income nations who are concerned that their local bank could misappropriate their funds.

One of the most important problem issues that Bitcoin could fix is to improve payment security. The standard credit card network basically employs the honor system and fraud detection only happens after transactions. Bitcoin can therefore be used to operate as the basis for payment systems that deal with fraudulent transactions in a much more sophisticated manner. For instance, if you are trying to push through a transaction through a bitcoin based android payment application, its interface could ask you to approve the transaction before submitting it to the bitcoin network.

The last thing and probably the most important considering the times that we live in is that Bitcoin is a fixed currency, which means that no government can force an inflation or deflation of the Bitcoin currency. As we saw with what happened with the United States government, the inflation of money caused a bubble collapse that resulted in the necessary saving of companies that would have otherwise destabilize the country. This is because the inflation rate didn't match the deflation rate on a much broader spectrum and this was influenced by big companies or at least that's what the conspiracies say. By having a currency that releases new coins every 10 minutes at a set rate for the next century, we can expect and understand the inflation rate that's going to affect us now and within a century.

In the next chapter, we will be discussing how bitcoin has risen over the years since it was founded to become the most valuable cryptocurrency in the world.

Chapter 3: Rise of Bitcoin

Thanks to Coindesk and Coinmarketcap, starting in the year 2013, we can actually see what happened to Bitcoin over that time.

The First Rise

In October of 2013, we saw Bitcoin rise in value dramatically, going from a few tens of dollars to nearly thousands of dollars. Speculators believe that the cause of this rise began earlier in the year with the Banking Crisis in Cyprus where the government forced banks to take the loss that they would incur. In order to avoid this, many smart individuals rushed to their accounts to pull out and push their money into Bitcoin, which is why you saw such a massive spike in Bitcoin. The reason why they did this is because of the anonymity and decentralized nature of Bitcoin, which meant that the government couldn't touch it. This only caused the price of Bitcoin to rise by a couple hundred dollars though before the price dropped again as hackers took to attacking some of the early Bitcoin exchanges. It seems that China caught wind of how important of an investment Bitcoin could be because it was China that brought the prices for Bitcoin up in October and this led to a surge of people trying to get their hands on Bitcoin so they could sell to China. It was during this month that Bitcoin first hit its' thousand dollar marke before climbing back down over time. It would never again go below $100.

The Second Rise

The second rise wouldn't be truly seen until the beginning of 2017, the year in which this book is written. While not as sharp as the first rise, the second rise is still continuing with two bubble-bursts while rising.

Starting in September of 2016, the price of Bitcoin has gone from $600 to nearly $4,800 by October of 2017. Both of the falls resulted in a near 50% loss with the first loss happening in July when the price dropped by nearly $500 and the next happening in September when the price dropped by nearly $1,000 before rising again.

Rising Profits

As more and more people join the network, the rarity of Bitcoin goes up, which means that the price for a BTC goes up. Due to the irregularity of Bitcoin, over time, there is actually a deflation of the cryptocurrency, given that only 21 million Bitcoins can ever be created. This number is less considering that some Bitcoins are lost due to people throwing old computers away when Bitcoin was worthless, loss of key phrases and a lack of care. There have been many stories where individuals disregarded their Bitcoin when it was worthless, only to find out it is worth thousands of dollars today. In some cases, there have been reports that these individuals have gone back to the junk yard to try and recover their old computers, only to find out that their Bitcoins are gone, worth potentially millions of dollars today.

The current Market Cap for Bitcoin is around $80,000,000,000 and this only happened over a decade. You could literally say that Bitcoin exploded into the market.

This explosion could not be possible without bitcoin miners availing the bitcoins to the market.

For a FREE course on how to buy your first Bitcoin, Litecoin, and Ethereum,

Get $10 worth of Bitcoin for free when you register today and invest $100

Chapter 4: Bitcoin Mining

Mining is Various

Bitcoin is created through a process known as Mining. One of the most noticeable parts about Bitcoin mining is that it is as confusing as can be whenever you're first trying to start your mining operation. Even if you are just curious about the technology, it can be confusing because of several different factors. You see, most people think there is only one way to mine Bitcoins because after all, there's really only one way to mine mineral ore and so it would only make sense that there's only one way to mine cryptocurrency but the truth is that there's more than one way. A lot of the confusion has to deal with just what goes into Bitcoin itself. There is more than one way to go about mining Bitcoin and this is where the confusion comes in. You primarily have three different options; solo mining, pool mining, and cloud mining. However, you actually have to understand how you get money from Bitcoin mining itself so let's cover that first before we cover the different ways you can mine.

Bitcoin Mining is a Reward Scheme

The first thing that you need to understand is that Bitcoin mining is actually not mining. It's one of those situations where it sounds like it could be one thing but it's really another thing. Essentially, the Bitcoin Network hands you a key that you need to work on in order to prove that the coin transaction occurred. This key is extremely complicated and the network measures it out so that it will take about 10 minutes to figure out the necessary hash function to validate the existence of those coins. Since Bitcoin transactions are happening all the time, these opportunities to validate coins is escalated to a height that you and I can go about mining these proof of work calculations. The first person who receives a correct version of the proof of work calculation is the person that receives the Bitcoins. There are a few different aspects to these calculations that cause problems with individual users though.

The Calculator Arms Race

You see, the average individual will have a computer that's capable of making billions of calculations every second and that's known as a gigahertz. Once people found that they could make money with this, the competition for the amount of calculations that are possible is significantly higher than it used to be. In the early days when cryptocurrency wasn't that popular, you could just utilize your CPU and generally make some Bitcoins every other day. As it grew in popularity, the calculations to solve the proof of work function became a lot more complicated and so it required a lot more processing power. The obvious first solution is to simply upgrade your hardware or upgrade the way in which you solve the equation. A lot of people spent money on processors because they were able to do the more complex equations at the time that Bitcoin was starting to grow in popularity, but they began to move over to GPUs once GPUs became rather powerful.

Why GPUs

GPU, also known as Graphics Processing Unit, is simply a much faster CPU. You see, with a regular processor, you only have maybe 8 to 32 cores depending on whether you have a mainstream processor or a server processor. Bitcoin miners would buy up as many 32 core server processors as they could possibly fit into a PC and since most server processors would only support up to a maximum of 2 server processors, there wasn't a lot of room for growth. That is until somebody had the bright idea to utilize GPU cores instead of CPU cores. You see, on a GPU you have thousands cores and we're getting to the point where there's going to be millions of simpler processors that handle chunks of calculations. Someone wrote the necessary algorithm to change the hash function so that it can utilize GPU power rather than CPU power. This happened only recently and was the primary cause for many shortages when it came to gamers wanting to buy a GPU to just play games. Since PC Gamers tended to buy the newest on the market and so did Bitcoin miners, the PC Gamers found that they were having a hard time locating top-of-the-line graphics cards because the Bitcoin miners invested a lot more money into purchasing the graphics cards as soon as they were on the market. Therefore, where a GPU Enthusiast that was a PC Gamer would normally buy a single graphics card the Bitcoin miner would buy 100 graphics cards. As you can see, this creates a shortage amongst the graphics cards and it increases the prices of the graphics cards in order to limit the wave of people that need them. However, due to the limitations of how many GPUs were available, we now came out with the technology called ASIC.

The New ASIC

ASIC stands for Application Specific Integrated Circuit and a lot of people are still really puzzled as to why this is better than a GPU. I'm going to come out and say that this is a battle between Generalized versus Specified. That may still be confusing, so let's use some search algorithms to see an example of where specification really matters. In computer science, we have Linear search and Binary search. Let's say we have a group of numbers from one to a hundred. If you don't know where twenty-five is, you would likely count from one to twenty-five. It is a slow and arduous task, but it will eventually get the job done. This is called Linear search and it is only useful when you have no idea where the numbers are organized such as : 1, 9, 89, 2. This is how a single GPU core is designed because it doesn't really know what is going to go where until it is done with a calculation. As you can imagine, such a Linear search is unreasonable when dealing with one person (a GPU core) and numbers that reach into the trillions. If you know the exact pattern of the numbers though, such as being ordered from one to a hundred, you can then run a Binary search instead. This is similar to how we see a Hash Function or Proof of Work function and an ASIC. A Binary search means that you continuously divide your search group in half and then see if it is more than one group and less than one group, going with the group that is less than. Therefore, on the search to twenty-five, you would divide the group in half, which would give you fifty, and see if twenty-five is more or less than fifty. Since it is less than fifty, we would throw out the more group and use the less group. Since twenty-five is the middle of the less group, we're done and it only took 2 steps instead of 25. ASIC is specifically built to only solve the Proof of Work function, which makes it extremely efficient there and useless everywhere else. A GPU is generalized so it can do the Proof of Work function *alright* but it can also do everything else *alright*.

Electricity

Now if you're wondering where the profit is made, you should be looking at the amount of electricity that it costs to actually run the hardware and software that will mine the Bitcoin for you. You see a lot of people like to jump into this big old pile of Bitcoin mining because they see the price tag on how much a Bitcoin is worth, but the truth is that mining it can actually be more expensive than the actual Bitcoin. Let's walk through an example. Let's say that a Bitcoin is worth $1,000. Let's say that it takes you about a year to get a full Bitcoin from all the mining that you do because you are likely to join a pool rather than solo mine. Let's say that it takes about 1 kilowatt an hour to run your mining operation at around $0.10 an hour. By running your system for a full 24 hours a day 365 days out of the year, you will have spent $864 on just the electricity. In other words, if you manage to make a Bitcoin that you can sell for $1,000, you will only have made about $140 in profit. This is what it means to judge whether your system is profitable enough for you to make any money off of it. Not only that, but the amount of money that it costs to actually buy the system necessary for the Bitcoin isn't even $140. Normally, such a system that would grant you a high enough reward that you could claim at least $1,000 a year is in the thousand dollars and higher range. This is why you need to make sure that it is actually profitable for you to mine before you go about doing it because you could easily dig yourself a hole without realizing it. The reason why some countries are building mining farms is because they have either built a system that runs entirely off of solar or the electricity costs so little that it only takes a very small portion out of their profit range.

One of the biggest players in Bitcoin Mining is Genesis Mining. Genesis mining works based on contracts. You can purchase different mining contracts, for example, Bitcoin contracts, which are an open ended contract. This means that the contract lasts forever as long as Bitcoin is profitable to mine. It is currently the most popular and profitable contract to date. Genesis mining promises a daily payout in any cryptocurrency of your choice. This form of mining is more profitable as there is no overhead costs such as electricity and maintenance.

For more information check out. https://www.genesis-mining.com/

For a 3% discount, use this code on ANY contracts: apS1YL

Pools

The primary way that people make money off of Bitcoin is by farming inside of pools. A pool refers to a collection of computers on a network that are all trying to solve the problem. The reason why this is the primary way is because everyone devotes their Bitcoin machines to solving a block code, the reward, and the first person who solves it splits the Bitcoin money amount amongst all the people inside of the pool. This means that it doesn't matter how powerful your system is; if your system is the one responsible for solving the code first then you hand out the Bitcoin reward in equal portions to everybody else. With that said, a lot of people don't see the benefit until they realize that finding the block code is different than solving the block. Someone else in your network might actually find the block code before you do but because your machine is more powerful than theirs, you are able to solve it. This is the primary benefit that comes with working in pools and there are several different pools to work in.

Worker

The term worker is used whenever people are talking about their processors and you set up a worker to run at a specific frequency so then you can actually get some calculations done. Essentially, whenever you hear the term worker, people are most likely talking about their entire system if they haven't set up several workers to take advantage of several different pools. Usually, the average individual will only have a single worker that's running on a single piece of hardware. However, if you build something like a Raspberry Pi Farm to handle multiple different processors then you are likely going to have as many workers as you do Raspberry Pi's.

How to Mine Bitcoin

Now there are several different ways you can actually mine your Bitcoins and there are benefits and downsides to each of them. The important thing to realize here is that almost all of them implement themselves in the same way. This is where I'm going to tell you how you actually mine your Bitcoins. First of all, you get a Bitcoin account and the most common place to start out is actually bitcoinmining.com or slushpool.com. If you do not want to mine Bitcoins yourself, you will need to go to a Bitcoin mining pool website like slushpool.com. The software that is commonly used for mining is BFGMiner, CGMiner, and libblkmaker. Many of these will lead you down a path of code found on Github, but navigating around a bit will lead you to version software. For simplicity sake, we're going to go down the path of Slush Pool.

1. You will need to setup an account with them like you would with any website really. You will have a user name and a worker name. For instance, TMkeg.worker1.

2. For Slush Pool, you will need either cgminer or BFGminer. With both of them, the directions are pretty much the same. Bfgminer.org will come out directly to a download page where you can download either Windows 32bit or Windows 64bit, or one of five supported linux distros. CGminer requires you to go to the Readme where you will find a section called

"Downloads" and following the link will lead you to a bunch of different versions of CGminer. Once you download either zip, you will extract it, find their executables, and run them.

3. Running the executable, you will be asked to enter 3 different items: URL, userID, and password. The userID is a combination of your Slush Pool username and worker name. The password is the password to the account. The URL, on the other hand, is found here: https://slushpool.com/help/get-started/getting started. The url is regional so there are five possible URLs you could enter, but it is up to you to choose the best one.

4. Once you enter that in, your CMD software is connected to the network and, provided you have an ASIC device, it will begin mining.

As you can see, this is relatively easy to implement once you get past all the jargon but the problem is that this is only one way of doing it. This is called pool mining and pools have requirements. You cannot join Slush Pool without having an ASIC device due to the high demands of today's Bitcoin market. I mean, we're talking about Peta hashes nowadays. To give you a clue about how huge this is, 1,000 Terabytes is a Petabyte.

Solo Mining

Solo mining is a little bit different but instead of pointing it at a pool, you point it at yourself. You see, all the pool is doing is pointing all the processing power into a single location so while somebody in Wyoming might have a farm of machines working on this, your computer will be pointed in the same direction as that person in

Wyoming. All it is doing is pointing your machines towards a single network access point. Therefore, in order to mine the Bitcoins yourself you just need to point it towards your device and so you're using the same miner software but you're setting it up with your own username, your own password, and your own pool. The username and password can be anything that you want but the pool is something different. The pool is your IP address and the port number that you set your GPU up on so that it doesn't confuse it with the GPU that your computer is using. In order to make this change so that your miner opens up to mining on your GPU automatically, you have to make a configuration file. For example, if I go into my cgminer-4.0.0 folder, I will find an example.conf file that I can open up with a Text Editor (not Word, but something like Notepad++) and see how my configuration file should be written. In order to find out what you need inside of it, you should definitely look at the code repository for your version of your miner. This is the hardest form of mining and the one with the least amount of payoff for anyone who doesn't have a football-sized Bitcoin farm.

Pool Mining

I've already explained how pool mining really works on a core level but here I'm going to actually elaborate on what I mean. You see, the people that you are pooling your resources with and the reason why it is called a pool is that it is handling all the network connections to solve bits of code. Imagine, if you will, a server farm that has a whole bunch of network connections interconnecting the servers but ultimately serves a singular purpose. This is what a pool does for the Bitcoin Network. This community has a singular network access point to the Bitcoin Network and you are part of a group of people (known as a pool) that is sharing that singular network access point. By doing this, the work that the Bitcoin Network requires of your machine is spread out amongst everyone who is a part of the pool. This is why when anyone manages to break the code inside of the pool, everyone inside of the pool gets a piece of the Bitcoin.

Bitcoin Mining Clouds

Now that you know what pool mining is, you might wonder what cloud mining is and how it is different from pool mining. It pretty much serves the same purpose but not everyone has access to the devices that are specific to certain types of pools. The ASIC requirement set forth by Splash Pool can't really be met by everyone who's trying to get into the industry just for the kicks of it. Anyone that's wanting a thousandth of a Bitcoin and can only afford their own computer will not want to buy a $600 - $1,000 machine. This is how Cloud mining was brought about because people who cannot pay for the device can rent one via the cloud so that they can just start up their own mining without having to do much. This ensures quality control, speed, and rate that also allows the company holding the cloud mining business model to expand and get more power. The problem is that some people will fall for traps when it comes to others who make it seem like they have a cloud mining operation but are just fooling people into believing that they have one while also collecting all the money that people invest into their business. After all, someone isn't going to notice that they don't actually have any Bitcoins until they submit a withdrawal request and then the person who owns the website can easily shut down the account without a reason and just evaporate into space.

Other Ways To Acquire Bitcoins

You already know that new bitcoins are created through the process of mining. But over the years, the bitcoin network has really grown and thus mining is now proving to become a very technologically complex task than it was since its inception. For most new users, it is virtually impractical to mine new bitcoins.

That is why there is the easier and better alternative to acquire bitcoins and that is by purchasing it from other people who already have them.

Buying bitcoins with your cash also has its own advantages. For example, it is not only easier than mining but it is also done privately and swiftly. This is because most exchanges will not demand that you to reveal your identity or give out critical information about yourself. Additionally, converting your money to bitcoin only takes a few hours and you are good to go.

There are a few ways to purchase such bitcoins. First of all, there are what we call Bitcoin exchanges. A bitcoin exchange is a digital marketplace that allows traders to sell or buy bitcoins using a variety of currencies. It is therefore an online platform that functions as an intermediary between the sellers and the buyers of any form of cryptocurrency.

One of the most popular exchanges includes Coinbase, which trades bitcoins for euros and US dollars. The trade is made all the more easier because the company has developed mobile smart phone apps to facilitate the exchanges. Another exchange is the Unocoin, which focuses solely on the Indian market. To trade using this exchange, you must register yourself with a PAN (Permanent Account Number) card. Last but not least is Circle. This exchange allows traders all around the globe to send, acquire and also store bitcoins. Basically,

41

the best exchange option depends on the country or region you come from. Basically there are many exchanges globally. This is a list of some of them and the mode of payment options that are allowed for each.

There are also websites that allow bitcoin traders who are interested in making bitcoin exchanges in person to find one another in their local areas. One of the websites that makes this possible is localbitcoins.com.

Lastly, most people can now buy and sell their cash for bitcoins using Bitcoin ATMs. It was not until the year 2013 that this new exchange mode was introduced. Basically, these ATMs were introduced to make it even easier and faster to sell or buy Bitcoins while also marketing further the idea of Bitcoin and therefore making it more accessible to many people.

It is recommended that you use the exchanges in the above list or conduct a thorough research before engaging in a trade through any exchange. This is because it has come to our attention that a growing number of sham exchanges are run by fraudsters whose aim is to acquire your personal information or details such as your digital key.

As you dip your feet into bitcoin mining or purchasing bitcoins, you will need a way of keeping/storing your bitcoins i.e. you will need a wallet. Let's discuss bitcoin wallets next.

Bitcoin Wallets

A bitcoin wallet is essentially what you might describe as a bank account for your bitcoins. This is because a wallet allows you to send, acquire and store bitcoins. Without a wallet, you cannot do any of these things. Therefore, a bitcoin wallet is the 1st step for you to start using bitcoins.

The function of wallets is to hold your secret codes (private keys) that allow you to spend bitcoins. In actual sense, it is not the bitcoins that you need to store and safeguard but rather your personal keys that allow you access to the bitcoins.

With this in mind, a wallet can either be a physical device (hardware), an application (software) or a website.

Hardware Wallets

It is any tangible/physical electronic gadget that is designed for the sole function of storing and safeguarding bitcoins. What makes hardware wallets to be secure than other wallet types is that you must connect the device to a computer, tablet or smartphone to spend them. Their purpose is to keep your private keys away from the susceptible internet connected devices. With hardware wallets, you can be sure that your private keys are well kept in a protected offline environment that is very secure even if the hardware were to be connected to a computer infected with malware.

This mode of generating and keeping private keys away from the internet makes sure that cyber criminals have absolutely no chance of sniffing their noses anywhere near your bitcoins. The only option for them is to physically steal the hardware itself, but still it will be useless for them because it is usually protected with a PIN security code that is only known to you.

The three most popular hardware wallets include Trezor, KeepKey and the Ledger Nano S. When you go shopping for a hardware wallet, it is advisable that you purchase one with a screen on it. This is because the screen offers extra security by not only displaying but also verifying crucial wallet details. Basically, this screen is more trustworthy than the information displayed on your computer monitor. One of the most popular hardware wallet is the Ledger Nano S. For more information, visit wonpublications.com/ledger

Hot Wallets

Hot wallets are the opposite of what we may refer to as 'cold storage' of bitcoins. You could compare cold storage of bitcoins to how banks move their client funds into a safe or vault instead of keeping them at the bank tellers' booth. In simple terms, a hot wallet is basically a software that you install on your internet connected device such as a tablet, phone or computer. Hot wallets are different to cold storage in that they are constantly connected to the internet. Hot wallets ensure that every bitcoin transaction keeps some sort of liquidity just in the event that there happens to be massive flood of withdrawal requests. Liquidity in this case can be likened to the cash reserves that any bank should have to make it convenient for the clients to access their funds at any time and point. This type of Bitcoin storage also ensures that you are in complete control of the security of your bitcoins. The only problem is that you store these coins on your computer that is connected to the internet and that leaves them more susceptible to cyber theft.

You could liken a hot wallet to your physical cash wallet that you carry around in your pockets because you can access it easily from there. You only use your cash wallet to keep some little cash but not all your life savings. In this case, hot wallets are used for temporarily storing small amounts of bitcoins where they can be withdrawn instantly if the need arises. They are also convenient if you like to make frequent payments. This means that receiving payments and spending your bitcoins using hot wallets is not only fast but it's also very easy.

As stated earlier, when using the hot wallet, you face the big risk of unrecoverable theft if it so happens that your device is hacked. Due to this vulnerability, you are advised to never keep huge amounts of bitcoin in your hot wallet. The hardware wallets are much more suited for that kind of task. Actually, many of the bitcoin losses suffered as a result of hacking can be attributed to the poor security practices of storing bitcoins in hot wallets.

Many trustworthy service providers that offer bitcoin withdrawal of any sort are known for keeping an extremely little number of bitcoins in their hot wallets. This enables them to carry out instant withdrawals of limited typical quantities. This means that they usually forced into a delay coupled with some manual job to carry out a bigger withdrawal because the funds have to be fetched from alternative storages.

One of the most common wallets for desktop computers is Electrum. This is a light weight software wallet that you can download and install on your computer. Released in the year 2011, Electrum is compatible with Windows, Linux and Mac operating systems. What makes it so popular is that it supports the various hardware wallets such as KeepKey and Trezor.

In case your computer hard drive gets stolen or corrupted, or worse still the whole computer is hacked, then the safety of your bitcoins is left hanging in the balance. This is the reason why you have to be well prepared for such happenings by installing a backup software. Moreover, it would also be wise if you try implementing some safety procedures such as a wallet address rotation. In a nutshell, it would be more safer to use such a wallet if you are tech-savvy.

You can also get wallets for smartphones such as Airbitz, breadwallet, mycelium and GreenBits.

Web/Online Wallets

These are basically web hosted wallets that you can access through your web browser just like you would with any other website. These websites store your private keys and you can access them from any place on planet earth provided that there is internet connectivity. Again, it is not advisable to keep a large number of bitcoins in your web wallet because the risk of cyber theft is high in such a platform. The best thing to do is to store them in cold storage.

Using the web based wallets to store your bitcoins means that you are entrusting third party companies to safeguard them for you. Therefore, you have to be wise enough to choose a reliable and trustworthy provider to store your bitcoins. Examples include: green address, BitGo and Blockchain.info.

The advantage with this kind of wallets is that the service providers take care of your overall wallet security for you including backing them up and implementing address rotations for you. You see, there is no online company that would like to have its reputation tarnished and risk losing clients because it is prone to cyber attacks. They will go an extra mile if need be to cement their status as the best in the business. It is up to you to choose whoever you think will be a reliable bitcoin wallet provider. And how exactly will you identify a secure bitcoin wallet? If they satisfy the following qualities, then they are trustworthy and reliable:

First of all, a reliable service provider puts great emphasis on security over anything else. And there are three ways they do this:

- If they are compliant with the DPA (data protection acts). Make sure that you contact your local data protection legislators and gauge the degree of compliance that that particular company offers.

- If they are able to conduct a device authorization test. They should be able to monitor your browser as well as the device you use so as to lock out any unauthorized access to your funds.

- If they a have a 2 factor verification before clearance. A trustworthy company will ask you for more authorization through an SMS to verify that it is really you logging in.

- And finally, if they encourage you to use strong passwords. If the service provider is as reliable as they say, they will usually warn you to always set strong passwords. For instance, using a 12 bit encryption password. Though some of the companies may be somehow lenient about such a security measure, that might not be perceived as a flaw on their part but it certainly takes off a few points to their security scoreboard.

Apart from security, you should also find an online wallet that offers an array of services for convenience. And one of the most important is probably the debit card as it makes sure that you develop further the manner in which you spend your money. For example, you may need to shop online and request for a delivery for a certain product. Due to the fact that finding a delivery service that accepts bitcoins is rare, you could solve that problem by using a plastic card. That's the beauty of debit cards. They can also enable you to verify accounts and also help you shop online without the need for ever going through a merchant who accepts bitcoins.

A reliable service provider is very transparent about the various costs they charge for withdrawals, transfers and processing deposits. Trustworthy companies go further with their transparency by making clear and open the details about the technicalities of new features. If there is any company that offers anything to the contrary, then you should just write them off as dodgy schemes.

Online wallets should be able to process speedy Bitcoin payments or payments using other currencies make sure you identify the number of countries where the wallet is fully functional and also take note of the limitations as well. As you research, look for the average time it takes to process payments. Arguably, the best way to research on this issue is to search for testimonials on independent media platforms such as Reddit.

And finally, make sure that you claim the full control over your bitcoins before you entrust your funds to a stranger online. When looking for a trustworthy wallet, ensure that they guarantee you the freedom to use it. This means that you should look for an online wallet that gives you secure and free withdrawals and money deposits wherever and whenever you need to. A reliable web wallet has nothing to fear or hide and they should be able to provide a continuous day or night access to the complete operational control of your funds. However, many companies will limit your withdrawal or deposits to only a few satoshi; the least amount being 0.0001 satoshi.

Paper Wallets

This is basically a printed piece of paper that holds information including the private key and a cryptocurrency address both of which are encrypted in the form of a QR code and can be decoded by a QR reader. Instead of saving those long series of characters on your computer drive that make up the private key, some people deem it fit to print the key instead and keep the paper in a safe place. Paper wallets are preferred to software or online wallets because like the hardware wallets, they are considered to be more secure for storing huge quantities of Bitcoin.

The advantage of using a paper wallet is that it is more or less like using a cold storage because it can't be connected to the internet and as a result, it cannot be hacked. Also unlike hardware wallets, they are a way cheaper alternative for cold storage.

Generating a non secure paper wallet is a rather simple task. Just visit the BitAddress website and generate your private key. Next click on the 'paper wallet' link and then print it. This is the wrong way to generate your paper wallet and DO NOT attempt to use follow it because it is non-secure.

The problem with this method is that you are connected to the internet as you carry out the process. And this means that people might be able to monitor whatever is happening on your screen. And this is true especially if you are using a computer running on Windows operating system because it is more susceptible to malware. Furthermore, if someone manages to hack the BitAddress website, he/she will have the chance to pick up all the private keys that people generate.

So what is the correct method? If you're truly determined to protect your bitcoins by generating a secure paper wallet, this is the due process to be followed. It may be a bit complex and tiresome but ultimately, it is worth every effort:

Make sure you download the essential tools and these include the BitAddress app, the Linux live app and the Ubuntu o/s.

Now install Ubuntu on your flash disk. This will delete everything else that is on the disk. Next launch the Linux Live and plug in the flash disk. Select the drive on your computer. if the icon does not appear, click refresh or hit F5 on the keyboard. Open the 'ISO/IMG/ZIP' folder and then click on the Ubuntu ISO file you downloaded in step 1. At this juncture, ensure that only the 'format the key oin FAT32' is highlighted. When all that is done, click on the lightning bolt icon to begin installation.

When installation is complete, now unzip the BitAddress and also copy it into the flash disk. The next and most crucial step is to **disconnect** the computer from the internet. Ensure that there isn't any remote access to your device. To run your PC using Ubuntu from the flash disk, hit F1 or F12 on your keyboard. A new page will appear. On it, click on the 'try Ubuntu option.

Now you have to make sure that your printer is synchronized with the new Ubuntu o/s so that you may be able to print. To do this, click on the 'cog wheel' and 'monkey wrench' icon to launch the system settings window. Select 'printers' then 'add'. Now you can synchronize your printer with the operating system. To check if it's working, print a test page.

The final step is to launch the BitAddress you downloaded and generate your own paper wallet on your PC's hard drive. To do this launch Mozilla Firefox, then right click and select 'open a new private window'. When the window appears, click on the address bar and type in:

File:///cdrom/bitaddress.org-master/

And press enter. On the next window, click Bitaddress.org.html. To generate the wallet, move the cursor until the reading on the top right comes to 0. Now select 'paper wallet' from the menu and then print it. Congratulations, you have now created your paper wallet. This process is considered to be a more secure because:

- You use the offline version of BitAddress meaning that it can't be hacked.

- You're using an Ubuntu operating system which is an 'out-of-the-box' strategy that is better equipped to fend off malware than Windows.

- And finally, you are disconnected to the internet while your private key is being processed.

Now that you know how to mine bitcoins and keep them secure in a wallet, the next part we will discuss is how to use bitcoins.

Chapter 5: How Bitcoin Is Used As Money

One of the first things that people think about whenever they think about Bitcoin is how it can be used as a currency rather than a stock item. While a great portion of the market is dedicated to the trading of Bitcoins with real currency, there is an equally large amount of individuals who utilized Bitcoins as actual currency so as to buy things such as a car or a coffee shop. There are a number of individuals who have purchased Lamborghinis and mansions solely by using Bitcoins.

Direct Transfer

One of the most obvious ways that Bitcoin is utilized as money is by directly transferring it to other Bitcoin users. Primarily, when a Bitcoin user wants to transfer over Bitcoins to another user they have to get their public key and utilize their digital wallets to transfer the Bitcoins over to that individual. You can store the Bitcoins on your computer and physically send them yourself but the process is rather complicated. Direct transfers are usually used simply because of how much easier it makes everything whenever you're trying to buy something such as a community couch or a car but the most common reason why someone would transfer Bitcoins is actually to purchase a service, but some services are not sold via Bitcoin and so some individuals will trade Bitcoins on a personal level so that they can bypass an online purchase scheme. An example of this would be a wallet that first converts the Bitcoins into the necessary currency that's going to be utilized by the service before transferring over the money so that even though the user has Bitcoins, the seller receives the currency that they are looking for.

Market Exchange

As we've already mentioned, some individuals decide to gamble inside of other cryptocurrencies besides Bitcoin and it's important to realize that you can exchange cryptocurrencies for other cryptocurrencies. If you think that a certain cryptocurrency is likely to be better than another, you can exchange your current cryptocurrency for that cryptocurrency that you're looking for. This doesn't happen a lot with the mainstream cryptocurrency as of right now but that isn't to say that it doesn't happen and that isn't to say that it won't happen in the future when other cryptocurrencies that are more trusted than Bitcoin come along to take over the market. Additionally, some users only trust a certain kind of cryptocurrency in an area so even though Bitcoin is trusted in most areas of the world, that doesn't mean that there aren't areas that refuse to accept Bitcoin and will only take certain cryptocurrencies that they produced themselves. As I said, this isn't really a common aspect to cryptocurrency market exchange but the honest truth is that it does happen.

However, a more likely scenario of a market exchange is if someone has had Bitcoins for a long period of time where they bought them at a significantly cheaper amount of money and now they're trying to pay out in order to get more currency such as the United States dollar or the Japanese Yen. This is the more common type of market exchange and it happens all the time when people buy low and then sell high, which is a tactic used by traders all over the world in the regular stock market. However, that doesn't mean that you're going to get the amount of money that you want all the time but the most common practice that people have is that they will buy Bitcoin when it's a very low price and wait until it's a very high price or until they see that they can make pennies on the dollar.

Services

As I've already mentioned, some individuals actually utilize Bitcoin as paying for a service like you would find on Amazon or Ebay. Due to the fact that there are no boundaries for Bitcoin, it becomes very handy when you live in a country that places large fees on money going in or money coming out or both ways. This means that individuals who are looking to avoid the nasty fees that normally come with exchanging foreign currency will likely go after the Bitcoin advantage of being a Global Currency. For this very reason, a lot of black market trades usually occur utilizing Bitcoin simply because it can go into a person's wallet without leaving a digital footprint behind it beyond the username of who owns the Bitcoin. That means that Bitcoins can be exchanged by literally handing over somebody's hard drive rather than holding onto millions of dollars inside of a briefcase. That isn't to say that unscrupulous people will use the anonymous aspect of Bitcoin but that is how it has become so infamous. Meanwhile, perfectly respectable people utilize this aspect on a daily basis simply because it is much easier to run exchanges by having a currency that isn't limited to borders.

Discounted Service

Another aspect that a lot of people have come to appreciate is that the value of Bitcoin increases over time with a rather High chance of success. Due to the fact that a lot of people realize that the value of Bitcoin increases over time, in order to get more customers that they can get a higher profit in the long run certain companies will actually provide you a discount if you utilize Bitcoins instead of real world currency so that they can gain more Bitcoins that will increase in value over time. This is a very small Niche part of the market but it does happen and a lot of people at take advantage of this. It is one of the best ways to utilize Bitcoin as a currency I rather than a stock option.

With all that in mind, the next chapter will focus on the benefits and risks that come with investing in bitcoins.

Chapter 6: Benefits And Risks Of Bitcoin Investing

Peer Value

The first attribute of Bitcoin that is both a risk and a benefit is that the value of Bitcoin is set by your peers. The risk is that your peers will no longer see any value inside of Bitcoin and so Bitcoin will lose any type of material worth, which means that if you invested thousands of dollars inside of Bitcoin then you would lose thousands of dollars as a result. However, that is also the benefit of Bitcoin. Since your peers can determine the level of value that's inside of a Bitcoin, this allows the market value of Bitcoin to become obscenely high at certain periods of time and then drop extremely low when everybody has been buying up for a while. This is how people generally make money and it's very close to gambling. This also increases the overall worth of Bitcoin due to the fact that the more people who are invested in Bitcoin means that there are more Bitcoins that are spread around and the value of Bitcoin goes up as a result. A good example of this is that Bitcoin used to only cost a total of $0 and now you can expect to spend over $14,000 to just get one Bitcoin. This is because the popularity of Bitcoin has gone up and this means that the overall value of Bitcoin has gone up as a result of this. Therefore, it's kind of like it could go wrong at any moment but you're hoping that it doesn't.

Sell Short

One of the benefits about Bitcoin is that you can sell short pretty quickly and this doesn't mean a lot unless you're used to trading in the regular stock markets. Selling short means that you can buy stocks or items when they are low and after waiting a short period of time, you can then turn around and sell those items to make a profit by raising those prices by a few cents or a few dollars. A lot of people don't think that trading like this can actually make you a lot of money but let's say that you have 100 Bitcoins and you bought them at $50 even, each. Now let's say that you waited for a couple of days and now those Bitcoins have become worth $60. That means if you decide to sell them at $10 extra a piece, you effectively made $1,000 in just a couple of days.

Sell Long

Just like you have selling short you also have selling long, which refers to the option of buying stocks when they are low price and selling them much later on in the life of the stock once the stock has reached a high enough price. A good example of this is buying stocks when they were maybe $5 to $20 a piece and trying to get as much of the stock as you possibly can. You wait a couple of years after you've bought this stock and suddenly you see that Bitcoin has made a bubble where you are watching the prices climb into the thousands of dollars. You can then automatically go straight into selling each of the stuff that you bought and easily make close to 15 to 22 and even $500,000 simply because you bought them at a low price when they first came out and waited until they became of suddenly high. This occurs whenever there's a bubble and we'll talk about this in a little bit.

Trust Issues

As I already mentioned, Bitcoin heavily relies on the trust that goes into it and since the professionals of the cryptology industry have certified that it would be incredibly difficult to hack Bitcoin, the value of

Bitcoin goes up. The problem is that if anyone manages to hack Bitcoin and gains the system then it all falls apart because the value of Bitcoin is reliant on how trustworthy Bitcoin network can be and if Bitcoin can't be trusted, then there is no more value inside of Bitcoin. Essentially, if somebody were to break the Bitcoin system then all of your Bitcoins would become almost useless overnight.

New Value Every Ten Minutes

People think that Bitcoin would become a stagnant market if it didn't constantly produce new Bitcoins or would become a novelty item that only the rich could afford but luckily for us, Bitcoin releases new coins every 10 minutes and it will do this for the next century. This means that the market will continuously get more coins that can be mined, found and utilized in the online space, which means that Bitcoin is likely to not be shortened by a lack of Bitcoins. The problem with this, even though it is a fantastic benefit, is that this means Bitcoin will not have an average value for a very long time. There are only so many dollar bills and we stop printing them unless we actually have to print and there are only so many European bills and they stop printing those if they have to, but Bitcoin is automatically set to release new Bitcoins without any interference whatsoever. This means that if Bitcoins become inflated, it is only by the market that they become deflated and this causes a huge problem in the economic view because since you can't control the deflation of a Bitcoin like you can a dollar, the crashes that come from a massive inflation of Bitcoin are much harsher than the crashes you might see in the United States dollar. For example, there have been two times recently within the past few years where the price of Bitcoin was cut in half. If the US dollar experienced something like this within two years, the US would be devastated and thrown back into a third world country.

Market Bubbles

This brings us to our last aspect when it comes to the risks and benefits of Bitcoin currency, which is to say that Bitcoin is very easy when it comes to market bubbles. A market bubble is whenever the inflation rate has risen so much that experts expect the bubble to pop and Bitcoin has quite obviously shown that it will pop. Bitcoin was worth tens of dollars a couple of years ago and now it's up to over 14,000 dollars. Originally, it began as being free and yet people are paying hundreds of dollars for a whole bunch of ones and zeros. The Bitcoin Market is a bit crazy but also understandable because it's almost the same as the markets for the US dollar and for the European dollar, but the Bitcoin isn't controlled by any singular government and runs on its own. This is why a lot of people are in this industry and like to trade Bitcoins back and forth. As you can tell, almost all the benefits that come with Bitcoin also have risks that come with Bitcoin. You'll see that is a very common trend when it comes to bitcoin currency exchanging.

If you would like to know more about cryptocurrency investing, check out my previous book, '*Cryptocurrency: 5 Expert Secrets For Beginners: Investing Into Bitcoin, Ethereum And Litecoin'.* In this book, I cover all the basics of cryptocurrencies and essential information experts use when investing into cryptocurrencies. Learn these tips today.

https://www.amazon.com/dp/B07571MSY5

Although I touched on the next topic earlier, I believe it is important to discuss it in detail so you know just how you can get bitcoins to get started if you haven't.

Chapter 7: Ways To Get Bitcoin

Buying Bitcoin with Fiat Money

The most obvious of all of these is to simply spend cash that you've earned doing whatever that you do on Bitcoins rather than mining for them or trying to sell a product for them. Once you buy Bitcoins, you can then do Bitcoin trading where you will either sell short or sell long and becomes almost identical to stock trading A common website where you can do this is Coinbase where you can buy the Bitcoins outright with money and then begin trading around. Coinbase is a simple exchange I would highly recommend for first time investors.

Selling Product for Bitcoin

Whether you're an online retailer or a coffee shop in Bangladesh, you can sell your products for Bitcoin. This is a primary way that individuals accumulate Bitcoins because many people simply seek out Bitcoins due to their worth and value. By staying on top of the market and having the ability to sell for Bitcoins, you not only get paid for the products that you're selling but the money that you receive actually grows in value rather than decreases in value, which is a common trend with some of the Fiat money that is around today. In addition to this, you can go out and sell on Craigslist or some other website that allows you to control what type of money you are requesting. This means that you can sell a car, a house, or anything that you could think up of for Bitcoins rather than paper money. This is a very common way to gather Bitcoins since a lot of people don't want to dive into Bitcoin mining and the amount of work it takes to actually retrieve Bitcoins from the system.

Work for Bitcoins

Don't forget that Bitcoin represents money and since money often represents labor, this means you can trade Bitcoins for labor and labor for Bitcoins. There are websites like Coinality that will allow you to trade your work for Bitcoins rather than United States dollars or any type of currency that you're used to working for. Due to the fact that Bitcoin is around $14,800 as of writing this book, you won't get a lot of Bitcoins by accepting some of these jobs and almost all of these jobs are freelance rather than full-time simply because of the nature of Bitcoins.

Debit or Credit cards

Buying bitcoins with credit or debit cards is one of the most common way to pay online. This is largely due to the fact that credit cards are a mode of payment that most people are familiar with and also it is of the easiest methods of buying bitcoins on the internet. The advantage of using this mode of payment is that you will receive your bitcoins immediately the verification process is complete. You can buy bitcoins anywhere in the world using your credit or debit card using Coinmama or CEX.IO. In European countries, you can but through BitPanda. Coinbase enables you to buy bitcoins with your credit/debit card in the whole of Europe, the USA, Singapore and Canada.

Coinbase in particular is the largest bitcoin broker in the world. You can buy up to €150 or $150 worth of bitcoins per week. Additionally, they charge a flat rate of 3.99% on all bitcoins you purchase using a debit or credit card. This fee is one of the cheapest for customers living in the United States and the European continent. Coinbase is offering free bitcoin worth €10 or $10 if you purchase bitcoin exceeding €100. You should know that coinbase only accepts Mastercard and Visa debit/credit cards as of now.

The process of buying bitcoins through Coinbase is simple. First you need to create and account and also add your personal details for login purposes. The site will ask you to upload a copy of your ID. Once that is done, click on your name situated on the top right corner of the window that appears. Now click on the 'settings' tab on the top of the window to launch a drop down menu. On that menu, click on "payment methods" then "add payment method" then credit/ debit card. On the window that appears, key in your credit/debit card details then hit 'enter'. You will receive a confirmation message that tells you that you have succesfully added a card. Now you are ready to buy your bitcoins. Hit enter again. There is a widget on the window that appears afterwards. Simply key in the amount of bitcoins you wish to buy then click "buy bitcoin instantly". Immediately after clicking, your bitcoins will be delivered to your preferred wallet.

Buying Through Bank Transfer Or Bank Account

In most countries, this is one of the best ways to purchase bitcoin. And these are some of the reasons. First of all, paying through bank transfers does not require a lot of fees and it is therefore cost friendly if you compare with other modes of payment. Another advantage is that this method allows you to buy huge amounts of bitcoins.

There are a few downsides however if this is your preferred mode of payment. It is usually a slow process because for instance in North America, a single bank transfer may usually take a maximum of 5 days before you receive your bitcoins. Again, it requires you to verify using your ID and therefore not a good choice if you are concerned about your privacy. You can buy bitcoins via your bank account using BitPanda in the USA, Gemini in the whole of North America and Coinbase in the USA, Europe, Singapore and Canada.

Buying bitcoins with PayPal

Purchasing bitcoins using PayPal is a complex and confusing process. But you shouldn't worry as I'll walk you through the entire process. The first thing you need to know is that PayPal utilizes the services of VirWox to buy bitcoins. It is impossible to buy bitcoins directly using PayPal. But VirWox is not technically a sort of Bitcoin exchange. This is because it is the equivalent of a market for second life lindens which is basically a form of currency used in the virtual world. The idea therefore is to buy SLLs (Second Life Lindens) from VirWox and then sell exchange them for bitcoins.

To buy bitcoins, you first need to open an account on VirWox by visiting the website. Once the page has been launched, key in your details to create an account. Most people get confused by a certain part named 'link to avatar' its not important though and you can leave it for now. Launch your email once you're registered to retrieve a temporary password that you will use to login to your VirWox account. On the window that opens, click on 'change settings' tab located on the left sidebar. This will allow you to change the password to your preferred password but ensure it is strong because it is your money you're dealing with. If you fail to change the password within a day, the accounted will be deleted. Once you've changed the password, click on 'deposit' located on the left sidebar. Scroll down until you find the option that allows you to key in the amount of money you need to deposit. Click on 'checkout with PayPal' button. Login to your PayPal and verify your balance. Now you'll need to exchange the money for

SLLs. To do this, key on the amount of money you want to exchange and hit 'enter'. On the top left, you will see your balance in SLL. Click on 'BTC/SLL' to enable the exchange to take place. Now key in the amount of BTC you want to buy and click 'next'. Now you should be able to see your bitcoins balance on the top left of your monitor.

Gambling

It's almost comical to know that whenever there's any type of money involved, you can almost guarantee that gambling has been on the path sometime during its creation. I don't think that there is a single money system on this planet that doesn't have gambling as a part of it. This is true of Bitcoin because you go on websites and gamble your actual money and they will pay you out in Bitcoins rather than currency. Due to the fact that there are no border limits to Bitcoins, it makes it much easier for gambling websites to give you Bitcoins rather than the currency denomination of your country.

Mining Altcoin for Bitcoin

Ironic as it may sound, it is actually easier in some cases to mine for alternative cryptocurrencies versus mining directly for Bitcoin itself. This is because there are a lower amount of individuals investing their time in the alternative cryptocurrencies and so those cryptocurrency values are still on the rise while Bitcoin is abnormally high. This means that you can race towards those Bitcoins with relative ease by using alternative cryptocurrencies that you can earn more of more quickly. As mentioned early, Genesis mining allows individuals to receive a payout in Bitcoin through different altcoin mining contracts. So this means you can enter a Litecoin or an Ethereum contract and get paid in Bitcoin.

The other thing we'll discuss is how bitcoin has opened up the space for the growth of other cryptocurrencies.

Chapter 8: How Bitcoin Has Allowed Other Cryptocurrencies To Form

Anonymous

The first thing that Bitcoin did that some of the other cryptocurrencies didn't do is that it anonymizes everyone. You can have whatever password that you want and you can have whatever username that you want; the only thing that matters to Bitcoin is that it has your username and front and your key in the back. While a lot of cryptocurrencies do this, it isn't actually a common trait with all cryptocurrencies. There were some cryptocurrencies that required your real name or wanted to implement a system that could utilize your real name so that it could only be tied to you. By anonymizing the currency, the currency can't be tracked by anything other than the Bitcoin Network and the people who retain the ledgers. A good example of why this is important is because the government could buy a ton of Bitcoins and effectively control the market by only releasing Bitcoins at a pace that it believes is appropriate. If the government knew, like China might, that you were the individual that held a certain Bitcoin that it didn't have then it could request that you send the government the Bitcoin. By utilizing any type of username that you wanted, you effectively gain anonymization, which prevents government control over Bitcoins in side of its' own borders.

Peer2Peer Validations

Part 1 of decentralized control means that all the people who serve as noted in the Network's serve as validations of Bitcoins in the Network's. In other words, no transaction can go on inside of the

Bitcoin Network where Bitcoin is utilized that isn't checked by thousands of other nodes that all have untampered with code. It's kind of like having an unlimited amount of notaries present for each and every transaction that occurs on the Bitcoin Network and this is far more powerful than any type of validation method used at a bank. In addition to this, due to the fact that the users of the Bitcoin networks are the Bitcoin users themselves this also means that there is no additional fee attached to validating transactions and keeping track of them. Essentially, it gets rid of the necessary jobs of a notary and a bookkeeper.

Decentralized Control

The second part of decentralized control is the fact that it is decentralized. This means that there is no one area that has more authoritative power over the economic system of Bitcoin and so no singular entity can control the influx or deflux of the system. This is very good for removing artificial bubbles that governments have created in the past with currency and so it creates a much more trusted Network amongst people who invest their time and money into the Bitcoin Network.

Controlled Release

This also means that there is a controlled release of Bitcoins rather than a fluctuating release like we've seen with much of the paper money currently in existence. Governments have blown up their amount of paper money being printed and this has caused governments like Greece to fall into a recession where there should not have been a recession in the first place. By having a controlled release base off of mathematical principles, every one can predict how the network will go in terms of growth and whether the network is dying or not.

Public Open Cryptology Methodology

The last part of this puzzle is the fact that the cryptology methodology involved with Bitcoin is open to the public for scrutiny. This means that other alternative coins are able to judge how Bitcoin handled the cryptology aspect of the coin and implement what it thinks is a better solution than Bitcoin.

All of these serve as a blueprint for each of the alternative coins that are currently out on the market and while those coins may have changed it slightly, this is the blueprint that's used for most of them. Since Bitcoin is so popular and so trusted but the value of Bitcoin and the Rarity of Bitcoin has gone up drastically, people have sought out ways to get access to other lesser-known cryptocurrencies so that it is not as difficult to farm them as Bitcoin currently is. The methodology of creating Bitcoin is easy to replicate and easy to change, but the access to Bitcoin has become more and more difficult, which means that the cap of Bitcoin is on the horizon. Even though there will be more Bitcoins to come out in the future, we cannot guarantee that we will have the technology to solve the blocks that are required on the Bitcoin Network and so alternative coins provide a option to switch over to a lesser-known network that isn't near its ending point. Additionally, because these lesser-known networks are easier to farm, people join in those networks so as to join what was effectively the Bitcoin rise in the beginning. Much of the people who are in the Bitcoin networks are people who found Bitcoin when it was small and wanted to explode it, now selling out as they reach thousands of dollars. Bitcoin was originally free for some users and as the value of

Bitcoin has gone up, people have wanted to get into the industry but the original people who were in the industry when Bitcoin was founded often payout so as to get the most amount of money that they possibly can and live a luxurious life. There are a lot of people who see the position that those people are in and want to be in those positions. All of these factors, the fact that Bitcoin is basically open to the public for recreation and redistribution as other names and the fact that it seems to be better when there are a lower amount of people help to increase the value that other coins have as Bitcoin seems to plateau.

Next, we will discuss another concept known as segwit.

Chapter 9: What is Segwit?

When you start looking at Bitcoin and Blockchain Technology, you'll start to notice there are actually a few different forms of Bitcoin. You might be wondering why these exist and which is real. There are multiple Bitcoin's, Bitcoin Cash and Bitcoin Gold and the 'normal' Bitcoin. To give you an idea of what the relationship is between the three Bitcoin's, we must need to understand what Segwit is.

Segwit, or Segregated Witness is the process by which the blockchain size of the network is increased. This is done through removing some transactions allowing faster and more transactions to occur. You can think of this like a memory card. The more full it is, the slower the memory card will be and the less memory can be held.

Soft fork vs Hard fork

So you might of heard this term before in cryptocurrencies, and if you haven't, that's okay, you'll hear it quite often. Soft forks and hard forks are exactly what it sounds like, a fork. It's essentially a brand out of the original network protocol. When the network requires a change, it goes through either one of these forks.

A soft fork is a *temporary* change to the system, an independent event occurring within the project. This is much like an update on the network.

A hard fork is a *permanent* change in the system and generally results in a creation of a new coin.

These forks occur due to divisions in the network, individuals' who want to support the current network and their goals, and individuals who want a change in the network. When the network requires a hard fork, this creates a 'new' coin, representing the 'new' project. You can see it like a pathway fork. If you're walking down the forest and you want to go to your friend's house, you'll take two different routes. Left

71

allows you to go to friend A's house and right allows you to go to friend B's house. Whichever route you take will result in two different outcomes. This is essentially what hard forks are about, two sets of individuals with two different visions.

It's important to distinguish the fact that hard forks still use the same blockchain network. The only real different is the vision of the project.

Bitcoin Cash

Bitcoin Cash was released on the 1st August 2017. The community behind Bitcoin Cash (BCH) wanted to solve Bitcoin's scaling problem. Because Bitcoin only recently gained popularity, the network has yet to meet the high demand necessary for the cryptocurrency. This has led to major issues in the Bitcoin network, primarily slower transaction times and high fees. The excess demand for the original Bitcoin means that more transactions must go through a smaller blockchain. Considering miners get paid to process these transactions, they process transactions faster to those who are willing to pay more, making fees absolutely crazy. This is the grand issue that Bitcoin faces and Bitcoin Cash addresses this by working to increasing its block size (currently 8MB), roughly 8x faster than Bitcoin, allowing more transactions to go through.

Today, BTH is considered a direct rival to the original Bitcoin (BTC).

Bitcoin Gold

Much like BCH, the introduction of Bitcoin Gold was not at all welcoming. In fact, it came under more scrutiny than BCH.

Bitcoin Gold (BTG) focuses on the miners. It's goal is to improve the mining capabilities of Bitcoin mining by allowing more people to mine and reduce the amount of powerful machines to do the mining. This will allow even more decentralization to occur as anyone will be allowed to mine, opening up mining to a wider user base.

Conclusion

Congratulations! Welcome to the end of this book! You're now an expert in Bitcoin, and while this may be the end of this book, this is definitely not likely going to be all that you learn about Bitcoin. Due to the ever-increasing Rarity of Bitcoin, there are likely to be several different markets that pop up so that the Rarity of Bitcoin doesn't begin to exclude other members from the Bitcoin community. There are currently 16 million Bitcoins on the market and there are only ever supposed to be 21 million. This means it's really important for the community to get together and collaborate on what to do so that Bitcoin doesn't end as fast as many people see it ending.

I hope you received valuable from this book, if you enjoyed this book, please leave a review on Amazon.com. Any review is greatly appreciated and I would like to thank you again for choosing this book. I strive to do the best I can and constantly revise the content.